CAMBRIDGE

B1 PRELIMINARY FOR SCHOOLS 1

WITHOUT ANSWERS

AUTHENTIC PRACTICE TESTS

Cambridge University Press
www.cambridge.org/elt

Cambridge Assessment English
www.cambridgeenglish.org

Information on this title: www.cambridge.org/9781108718356

First published 2019

20 19 18 17 16 15 14

Printed in Great Britain by Ashford Colour Press Ltd.

A catalogue record for this publication is available from the British Library

ISBN 978-1-108-65229-2 B1 Preliminary for Schools 1 Student's Book with answers with Audio
ISBN 978-1-108-71835-6 B1 Preliminary for Schools 1 Student's Book without answers
ISBN 978-1-108-71837-0 B1 Preliminary for Schools 1 Audio CDs (2)

Contents

Introduction

This collection of four complete practice tests contains papers from the *Cambridge English Qualifications B1 Preliminary for Schools* examination. Students can practise these tests on their own or with the help of a teacher.

The *B1 Preliminary for Schools* examination is part of a series of Cambridge English Qualifications for general and higher education. This series consists of five qualifications that have similar characteristics but are designed for different levels of English language ability. The *B1 Preliminary for Schools* certificate is recognised around the world as proof of intermediate level English skills for industrial, administrative and service-based employment. It is also accepted by a wide range of educational institutions for study purposes.

Cambridge English Qualifications	CEFR Level	UK National Qualifications Framework Level
C2 Proficiency	C2	3
C1 Advanced	C1	2
B2 First for Schools	B2	1
B1 Preliminary for Schools	B1	Entry 3
A2 Key for Schools	A2	Entry 2

Further information

The information contained in this practice book is designed to be an overview of the exam. For a full description of all of the above exams, including information about task types, testing focus and preparation, please see the relevant handbooks which can be obtained from the Cambridge Assessment English website at: **cambridgeenglish.org**.

The structure of *B1 Preliminary for Schools*: an overview

The *Cambridge English Qualifications B1 Preliminary for Schools* examination consists of four papers:

Reading: 45 minutes
Candidates need to be able to understand the main points from signs, newspapers and magazines and use vocabulary and structures correctly.

Writing: 45 minutes
Candidates need to be able to respond to an email and to write either an article or a story.

Listening: 30 minutes approximately (plus 6 minutes to transfer answers)
Candidates need to show they can follow and understand a range of spoken materials including announcements and discussions about everyday life.

Speaking: 12–17 minutes
Candidates take the Speaking test with another candidate or in a group of three. They are tested on their ability to take part in different types of interaction: with the examiner, with the other candidate and by themselves.

	Overall length	Number of tasks/parts	Number of items
Reading	45 mins	6	32
Writing	45 mins	2	–
Listening	approx. 30 mins	4	25
Speaking	12–17 mins	4	–
Total	approx. 2 hours 12 mins		

Grading

All candidates receive a Statement of Results and candidates whose performance ranges between CEFR Levels A2 and B2 (Cambridge English Scale scores of 120–170) also receive a certificate.

- Candidates who achieve **Grade A** (Cambridge English Scale scores of 160–170) receive the Preliminary English Test certificate stating that they demonstrated ability at Level B2.
- Candidates who achieve **Grade B** or **C** (Cambridge English Scale scores of 140–159) receive the Preliminary English Test certificate at Level B1.
- Candidates whose performance is below B1 level, but falls within **Level A2** (Cambridge English Scale scores of 120–139), receive a Cambridge English certificate stating that they have demonstrated ability at Level A2.

For further information on grading and results, go to the website (see page 5 for details).

Speaking: an overview for candidates

The Speaking test lasts 12–17 minutes. You will take the test with another candidate. There are two examiners but only one of them will talk to you. The examiner will ask you questions and ask you to talk to the other candidate.

Part 1 (2–3 minutes)
The examiner will ask you and your partner some questions in turn. These questions will be about your personal details, daily routines, likes, dislikes, etc. You will only speak to the examiner in this part.

Part 2 (2–3 minutes)
The examiner will give you a colour photograph to talk about. The photograph will show an everyday situation. You will be given one minute to describe what you can see in the photograph.

Part 3 (3 minutes)
In this part, you and your partner will talk to each other. The examiner will give you a card with some illustrations on it that are connected to an imaginary situation. You will then be given about two minutes to discuss ideas with your partner. During the discussion, you should make and respond to suggestions, discuss alternatives, make recommendations and negotiate agreement with your partner.

Part 4 (3–4 minutes)
The examiner will ask you and your partner some questions about the topic introduced in Part 3. The questions will focus on your likes, dislikes, habits and opinions. The examiner will either ask you to respond individually to the questions, or to discuss them with your partner.

Test 1

READING (45 minutes)

Part 1

Questions 1–5

For each question, choose the correct answer.

1

A There are three badminton sessions a week at the new club.

B The new badminton club can only have 18 members.

C Students need to decide quickly whether they want to join the new club.

2

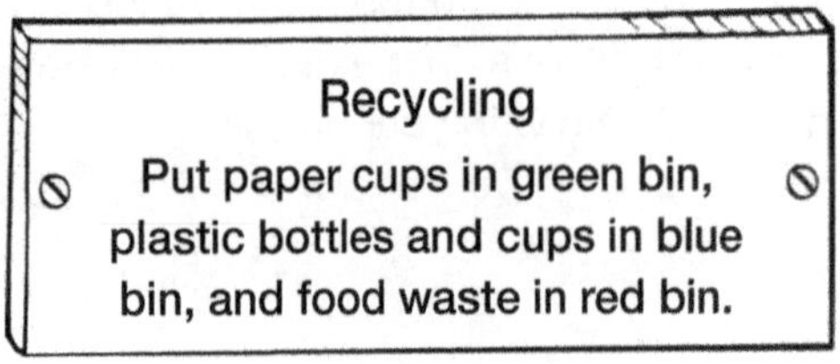

A Unfinished burgers should go in the red bin.

B Only bottles should go in the blue bin.

C Plastic cups should be put in the green bin.

3

Daniel's mother is texting him to

A ask Daniel to do her a favour.

B complain that she has too much to do.

C apologise for forgetting to tell Daniel something.

4

From :
To :

Summer reading challenge for library members aged 12 – 18. Choose from the attached book list. You'll get a certificate for each book you read and a prize if you read six.

A People can read any book from the library as part of the reading challenge.

B Only certain people can take part in the reading challenge.

C Everyone who takes part in the reading challenge will receive a prize.

5

OUTDOOR COURTS

All players need T-shirts, shorts, sun hats and proper tennis shoes, apart from under-10s, who may wear their gym shoes.

No entry for students wearing the wrong shoes.

A Younger players must have proper tennis shoes to play here.

B Only older students are allowed to play on these courts.

C All players must wear the correct kit when using these courts.

Part 2

Questions 6–10

For each question, choose the correct answer.

The young people below are interested in joining a dance or drama group.
On the opposite page there are descriptions of eight dance and drama groups.
Decide which group would be the most suitable for the people below.

6 

Maiko loves dancing and wants to learn new dance styles quickly. She'd like to meet successful dancers and also take part in competitions.

7 

Marta and her younger sister would like to join an acting group at the weekend. They haven't done anything like this before, so their mum wants to go with them at first.

8 

Eliana's quite nervous so would like the possibility of some drama training on her own at first. She's free during the week and hopes to act in a play one day.

9 

Henri is an experienced dancer who enjoys entering competitions. He wants to concentrate on jazz dance and improve his drama skills too.

10 

José wants to perform in plays, and is interested in joining an acting course run by professionals with a diploma at the end.

Dance and drama groups

A Let's go!
We offer classes for advanced dance and drama students who want to develop their talents to a really high level. Our expert teachers will work with you on your acting and your preferred dance style so that you are ready to compete against the best!

B Mouse House
We welcome all levels of ability and experience, and offer drama classes for children of all ages, led by professional performers. The activities are fun and great for building self-confidence, so you are soon ready to enter competitions. We meet every Saturday and parents are welcome to wait in the hall.

C The Phoenix Group
With us, you'll take part in weekend drama workshops and receive a free ticket per term to watch a play at the local theatre. You'll have opportunities to perform to the public throughout the year. No experience is necessary, but you will need to book a term in advance.

D Monsters DC
This group is for young people under 16 who want to develop their acting ability, or for more experienced actors who want to teach others their skills. All our members are encouraged to take part in our annual show, and every month you can meet successful actors and get their advice on a career in acting.

E Peppermint Performers
Working with experienced theatre directors, you'll learn performance skills through a year-long programme of workshops. The first term is a series of skills-based sessions covering a range of different performance styles, with certificates for successful students. In future terms, you'll take part in plays performed for the general public.

F Moon Productions
In our classes, we teach jazz, tap and street dance, and you'll soon be creating your own dances. We hold contests against other clubs and put on displays for parents every summer. Want to find out what a life as a professional dancer is like? Every term we invite a star to talk about their career.

G The Focus Group
Classes are available every evening. You'll receive excellent training in dance and drama, and develop techniques and performance skills in no time. One-to-one tuition is offered, and it's possible to work towards a certificate. You'll also have the opportunity to take part in a professional play.

H Bubble Company
Just come along with your friends and we'll do the rest. There's no need to have any experience, and we provide all the costumes and special dance shoes if you need them. We run small hour-long classes in dance or drama every evening after school, and family members are welcome to stay and watch.

Part 3

Questions 11–15

For each question, choose the correct answer.

My name's Martin Cabello and I'm a young photographer. Taking photographs was always my favourite activity as a child. And when I was 15, I felt that if I wanted to take my hobby to the next level, I had to do something special. So I decided to start a personal project: I would take one photograph every day for a whole year of my life. I knew that many other young photographers before me had done the same thing, but it seemed like a really great idea, and so I started.

After a few weeks, I decided to put these photos onto a website for young photographers because I was keen to create a photo diary, and also to have the chance to show other people my photos. I was amazed to discover that there were others who liked the way I saw and photographed things. I was also enjoying photographing a wide range of subjects. Then someone suggested that if my photographs all had a common topic or idea to connect them, my project would be even better – and I agreed.

So I began to concentrate more on taking photos of nature scenes, especially of birds and the sky. A lot of them were black and white photographs, which was very different to what many other young photographers were doing – they were all taking colour photos. As a result, I sometimes had doubts about my project, and I almost gave up several times. In the end, however, I trusted my own feelings, and became more confident about my photographic style and choices.

One day I showed my project to my art teacher at school. She told me about a national photography competition for people my age. So I entered some of my photos, just for fun. I'll never forget the moment when the judges told me that I had won first prize; I was so happy, as my project meant so much to me. It was the first time I realised that maybe my photography really was good, and that I might actually be able to work as a professional photographer. I now have my own photography studio and I've never regretted my career choice.

11 Martin started his project because he wanted to

- **A** influence other photographers.
- **B** try an original idea of his own.
- **C** take a lot more photos than he had before.
- **D** develop his photography further.

12 What happened after Martin put his photos on the website?

- **A** He became more interested in other photographers' pictures.
- **B** He was given some advice to improve his project.
- **C** He decided that his photos weren't good enough.
- **D** He discovered that the website wasn't the best place for his photos.

13 How did Martin feel when he took his first nature photos?

- **A** He wasn't sure that he was doing the right thing.
- **B** He was certain that the photos would be better in colour.
- **C** He was anxious about what others would think.
- **D** He was worried that his photos might not be interesting.

14 How did winning the competition affect Martin?

- **A** He realised how enjoyable competitions can be.
- **B** It helped him to make a decision about his future.
- **C** It gave him the opportunity to meet more young photographers.
- **D** He started putting more effort into his photography.

15 What would be a good title for this text?

- **A** My favourite websites for sharing photographs.
- **B** The best way to become a successful young photographer.
- **C** How a photography project changed my life.
- **D** Why more photographers should take pictures of nature.

Part 4

Questions 16–20

Five sentences have been removed from the text below.
For each question, choose the correct answer.
There are three extra sentences which you do not need to use.

Ballet for children and teenagers

It can take a long time to reach a professional level in ballet, so most dancers begin their training very young. It is essential that very young dancers learn the ballet movements properly right from the beginning. **16** ______ This is because it is usually more difficult to change old habits than to learn new ones.

The first thing that young children who are interested in learning to dance often do is attend creative movement classes, where they can practise basic skills like jumping and turning, and just have fun. **17** ______ In addition, some people recommend that they should learn either to sing or play an instrument.

Young people who decide they want to have a ballet career can attend a dance school. Here, students not only study normal school subjects but also do daily dance training. **18** ______ And the whole dance-school environment is set up to support the young people's artistic development; it allows them to focus on their dance more easily, and prepares them for their future. But how can a young dancer and their parents tell which dance school is the most suitable? **19** ______ The older students taking part in it should clearly have more highly-developed ballet skills than the younger dancers.

By the time they are 16 or 17, many ballet dancers are entering ballet competitions and taking classes at professional studios. **20** ______ It is important for young dancers to know how well they are doing, because the dance world is very competitive and the training hard; not everyone makes it to the top.

A	For all these reasons, they enjoy meeting other dancers.
B	Listening to different styles of music also helps.
C	Travelling long distances to dance schools can be tiring, too.
D	Attending one of their public performances is a good way of finding out.
E	If they develop poor technique, they may have problems later on.
F	Few people know where to find them.
G	This allows them to compare themselves with teenagers from other schools.
H	That means they do not waste time travelling from home to dance classes.

Part 5

Questions 21–26

For each question, choose the correct answer.

Living on a boat

Fourteen-year-old Jon Atkins hasn't had a typical childhood. His parents had always intended to buy a boat and sail round the world, and when Jon was eight they did **(21)** .... that. When they first told him of the plan, Jon felt sad about **(22)** .... his friends, but also excited because of the adventures he would **(23)** .... Since then, Jon has sailed over 8,000 km and **(24)** .... that he loves living on a boat.

The boat has two sleeping cabins and Jon's cabin has just enough **(25)** .... to sit up in. In the main cabin there's a desk where he studies every day, as he needs to continue his education. Although he doesn't have any teachers, he doesn't think his lifestyle will **(26)** .... his future choices. He plans to become a ship's captain, and is certain that life on a boat is excellent preparation for this.

21	**A** definitely	**B** exactly	**C** certainly	**D** absolutely
22	**A** departing	**B** moving	**C** remembering	**D** leaving
23	**A** have	**B** set	**C** do	**D** make
24	**A** expected	**B** discovered	**C** imagined	**D** believed
25	**A** area	**B** size	**C** space	**D** place
26	**A** contain	**B** fix	**C** limit	**D** control

Part 6

Questions 27–32

For each question, write the correct answer.
Write **one** word for each gap.

My city

by Harry Salter

Do you live in a nice place? I do! The city **(27)** .... I live is called Bristol, and it's in the south-west of England. It's not very big, but there are loads of things for teenagers to do here.

(28) .... you're interested in television, you should go to the Bristol TV and Radio Studios. On the tour of the studios, you can have a go at presenting and appear **(29)** .... your own radio drama.

Or if you're into sport, why **(30)** .... try canoeing? The best place is a very pretty local section of the Kennet and Avon canal. It connects Bristol to London and it **(31)** .... built in the early 18th century, so you can experience some local history at the same time.

These are just two **(32)** ....the many things you can do here. It really is a great place.

WRITING (45 minutes)

Part 1

You **must** answer this question.
Write your answer in about **100 words** on the answer sheet.

Question 1

Read this email from your English teacher Mrs Hallam and the notes you have made.

EMAIL

From: Mrs Hallam

To: All students

Subject: School talent show

Dear Students,

I'm planning to organise a school talent competition. Students taking part in the competition can sing, dance, play a musical instrument or perform in some other way. — *Good idea!*

The talent show could be for students of all ages, or just for students over 15. Which do you think would be better? — *Explain which is better*

I think that some parents should judge the competition. Do you agree? — *Tell Mrs Hallam*

And finally, what prizes do you think the winners should receive? — *Suggest …*

Please reply soon.

Beatrice Hallam

Write your **email** to Mrs Hallam using **all the notes**.

Part 2

Choose **one** of these questions.
Write your answer in about **100 words** on the answer sheet.

Question 2

You see this announcement on an English-language website.

> **Articles wanted!**
>
> **Sport and exercise**
>
> Are there enough sports activities for young people to do in your area?
> Do you think it's important for young people to do sport and exercise?
>
> Why?
>
> Write an article answering these questions and we'll publish the best ones.

Write your **article**.

Question 3

Your English teacher has asked you to write a story.
Your story must begin with this sentence.

Lois smiled as she put the tickets in her pocket and walked out of her house.

Write your **story**.

LISTENING (approximately 30 minutes)

Part 1

Questions 1–7

For each question, choose the correct answer.

---

1 What will they eat for dinner?

A

B

C

2 Where did the police find the stolen statue?

A

B

C

3 How did the mountain climbing group celebrate their success?

A

B

C

4 What does the boy think his friend should buy?

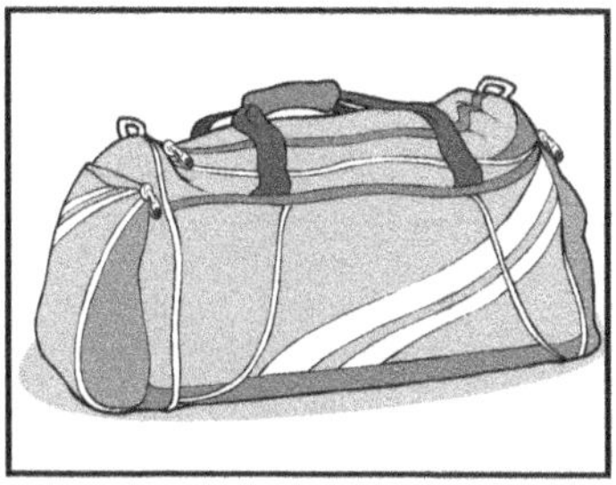
A

B

C

5 What's the girl's holiday job?

A

B

C

6 How are the friends going to get to the cinema?

A

B

C

7 What are they going to study in their next lesson?

A

B

C

Part 2

Questions 8–13

For each question, choose the correct answer.

---

8 You will hear two students talking about a history book.
They agree that

A it should be shorter.

B it helps with their schoolwork.

C it has some information missing from it.

9 You will hear two friends talking about their lunch break at school.
They both plan to

A finish their homework.

B eat the same food.

C play games on their phones.

10 You will hear two friends talking about a film they have seen.
What does the boy say about it?

A It made him laugh.

B He guessed the ending.

C The acting was bad.

11 You will hear two friends talking about a school trip.
They agree that the trip was

A not long enough.

B quite expensive.

C badly organised.

12 You will hear a boy telling his friend about a science lesson with a new teacher.
What does the boy say about the new teacher?

A She asked a lot of questions.

B She made the lesson fun.

C She knew her subject well.

13 You will hear two friends talking about where to have a party.
Why do they prefer the park to the sports club?

A There's lots of space.

B They can play games there.

C It's in a convenient location.

Part 3

Questions 14–19

For each question, write the correct answer in the gap. Write **one** or **two words** or a **number** or a **date** or a **time**.

You will hear some information about a talk at school by a writer called Marcia Wilson.

Talk by Marcia Wilson

Day of Marcia Wilson's talk: **(14)** ....

Name of her new book: The **(15)** ....

Where she will talk: in the **(16)** ....

Time the talk begins: **(17)** ....

Cost of buying her book at school: £ **(18)** ....

Useful website to look at: www. **(19)** .... .uk

Part 4

Questions 20–25

For each question, choose the correct answer.

You will hear an interview with a girl called Anna Taylor, who is a champion cyclist.

20 Anna became interested in cycling because

A she was bad at other sports.

B she had a friend who encouraged her.

C she enjoyed her first experience of it.

21 How does Anna practise her cycling as well as do her schoolwork?

A She studies hard in the evenings.

B Her teachers give her extra time.

C She has to miss some classes.

22 What does Anna say about track cycling?

A It is faster than road cycling.

B It is harder to learn than road cycling.

C It requires more power than road cycling.

23 What does Anna say about cycling with teammates in road races?

A She likes the feeling of support around her.

B She likes learning techniques from others.

C She likes laughing with friends at difficult times.

24 Anna says that at her last road race she was

A upset by the behaviour of her competitors.

B surprised by what happened at the beginning.

C disappointed by a teammate's performance.

25 Anna thinks people who want to be champion cyclists should

A train hard every day in order to be the best.

B do lots of other sports to help them keep fit.

C spend time trying different activities.

Test 2

READING (45 minutes)

Part 1

Questions 1–5

For each question, choose the correct answer.

1

Derek is contacting Ella to

A suggest they change a plan.

B invite her to meet his aunt.

C remind her about an arrangement.

2

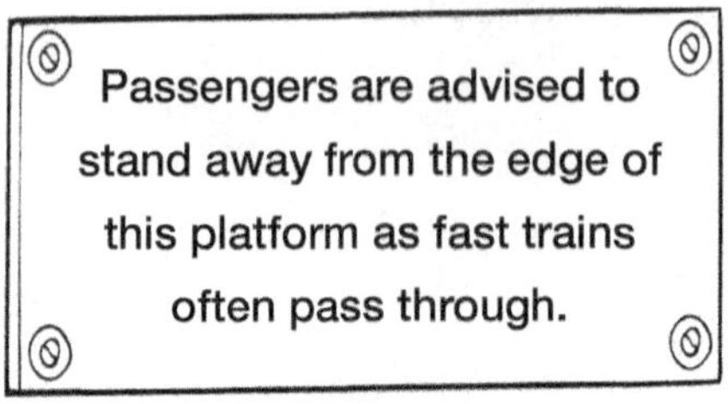

A People can get information about fast trains on this platform.

B People waiting for a fast train should not stay on this platform.

C People on this platform should not get too close to the railway line.

3

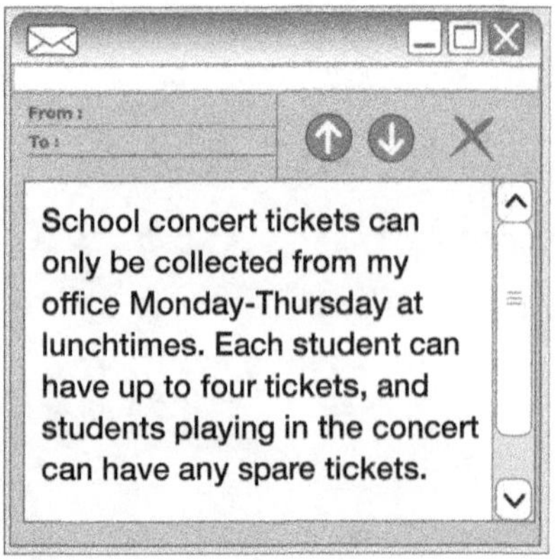

A Students not playing in the school concert will get fewer than four tickets.

B Students are not able to pick up concert tickets at any time they like.

C Every student will have the same opportunity to get extra tickets.

4

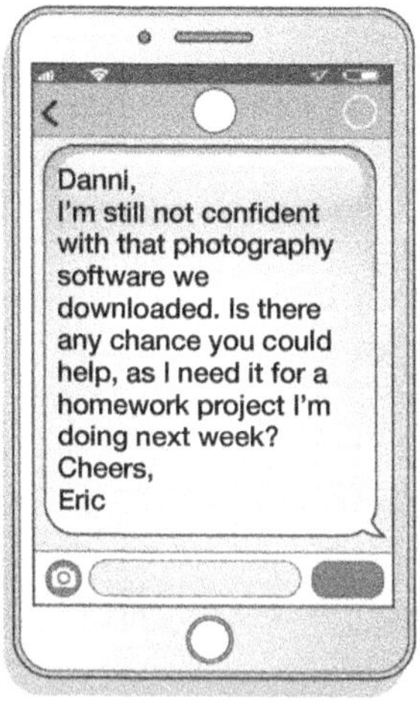

Eric wants Danni to

A lend him some software.

B download some software for him.

C show him how to use some software.

5

School lunch rules

Pupils are requested not to leave the table as soon as they have finished, but to remain in their seats until a teacher has said that they may go.

A Sit down at the table when the teacher asks you to do so.

B Wait until the teacher has finished eating before leaving the table.

C Stay at the table unless the teacher tells you that you can leave.

Part 2

Questions 6–10

For each question, choose the correct answer.

The young people below are looking for a day out with family or friends.
On the opposite page there are descriptions of eight outdoor activity centres.
Decide which activity centre would be the most suitable for the people below.

6 

Julian wants to take pictures of wildlife but needs some advice. He likes to be near water and also wants somewhere that has outdoor eating facilities.

7 

Marcie and her mum want to spend a day in a forest and get some exercise at the same time. They would like to be told about the wildlife there, and enjoy snacks and refreshments in comfort.

8 

Mohammed wants a day full of activities including something that involves his two main interests, sport and animals. He also wants to try an art class and to stay for a night-time activity too.

9 

Maria wants to be able to read about the wildlife and also to take pictures of trees and hills. She loves being outdoors and would like to try a watersport of some kind.

10 

Ivan and his dad want an activity that involves seeing and hearing wildlife. They also want to do an adventure sport and to try food that comes directly from the local forest.

Outdoor Activity Centres

A **Bennachie Park** is an area of great natural beauty and very popular with photographers and artists. There is a sculpture trail through the forest, and a famous waterfall, and both of these can be reached on foot or by mountain bike. You can hire bikes from the Visitor Centre.

B **Wilder Forest** has a huge web of paths for walkers, runners and mountain bikers, and you can also do horse riding (booking required). There are beginners' sessions available in drawing nature with painter, John Small, and a new event that starts after dark will introduce you to the stars.

C **Strathmoor Forest Park** is very popular both with people who want to enjoy relaxed walking and with birdwatchers who come to see rare birds found only in Strathmoor. There's a small café, and several picnic sites for those who prefer to bring their own food.

D **Thornielee Park** is a wonderful place for a family day out with fantastic hilly walks, two large lakes, and many picnic sites where you can enjoy the views. It's popular with animal lovers and has daily bird-photography drop-in sessions with our expert, Sarah Wallis.

E At **Glengarry Forest**, there is a new storytelling event for children, called 'Deep in the Forest'. Then there are many regular activities and events, including the ever-popular horse riding and night-time cycling with torches. The food at the Visitor Centre café is excellent and won a prize last year.

F If you love nature, **Innerleithen Forest** is for you! There are several rare kinds of animals and birds, and a daily talk on them from an expert at the Visitor Centre. You can also get cosy in the café, which serves cake and warm drinks. Many people bring mountain bikes or you can hire them and go around the forest trails.

G **Boden Forest** is excellent for walking and running, and there's also a 10-metre cliff face with climbing classes for beginners. A regular birdsong event takes place, including birdwatching from inside a special hut. Very popular for lunch is the food stall, serving mushrooms grown there and fish from Boden.

H **Kiroughtree Park** has everything from a visitor centre – where you can pick up a free guide full of information about the plants and animals there – to a wonderful lake, where you can have a go at sailing. Short landscape photography sessions are also available.

Part 3

Questions 11–15

For each question, choose the correct answer.

Rock the Planet

Music journalist Nick Hilman meets young actors from this popular musical show.

Rock the Planet, a musical show where actors also have to be really good musicians, opened in London last year, after five years in the USA, where it was voted 'Best Musical' four times! But doing the show with an all-British cast of actors was challenging. The UK puts more limits on how many performances young actors can do weekly – in the USA, they're allowed to do more shows. Because of this, twice as many actors were required here. Luckily, the director found plenty of talented UK-based actors, and they've just won their first 'Best Musical' award. Although the theatre in London is bigger than the US venue, it's been full every night, with everyone wanting to hear the songs that first became popular in America.

I met 11-year-old Jamie, one of the show's actors. 'It's brilliant that I get paid to play,' he said, 'especially a beautiful and expensive Gibson guitar.' He told me how busy the young actors are. 'We have normal school lessons each day at the theatre. While the teacher's great, I miss my old school mates.' And what do they think of the show? 'Well, my whole class came! The theatre does special deals on tickets for schools. They absolutely loved it and that made me feel really confident. My parents come when they can, but it's expensive for them,' he explained.

When I said I also play guitar, Jamie found a spare one and invited me to play along with him and the other young actors. We played *Days*, a song I wasn't familiar with. Jamie took me through it and I was very pleased with myself when I finally got it right. I was impressed by Jamie's ability and wished I had similar skills. I was just trying to keep up and was glad the show's director wasn't there to hear my mistakes!

While the young actors were already musicians, with some playing several instruments, none had played in a band before. Fortunately, they've found it pretty easy. Jamie admitted that the hard part was appearing natural when they first performed together. They were concentrating so much that they forgot to smile!

The show's on in London for another year, and is well worth seeing.

11 What is the difference between the shows in the UK and in the USA?

A Fewer young actors were needed in America.

B Brand new songs have been included in the UK.

C The UK show has won more prizes.

D Audiences were bigger in America.

12 What does Jamie say about working on the show?

A He's glad that his family come daily to support him.

B He's embarrassed when his friends come to watch him.

C He's delighted that he's doing something that he loves.

D He's anxious about the amount of schoolwork he's missing.

13 How did the writer feel about playing music with the actors?

A surprised that he sounded as good as Jamie

B satisfied that he had learned a new song

C happy because they played his favourite tune

D excited to be playing in front of the director

14 What did the actors find difficult about performing in the show?

A having to play their instruments with other people

B learning to play many new instruments very quickly

C remembering the different songs they had to do

D looking relaxed when they were playing on stage

15 What would an advertisement for the show say?

A Come and enjoy this wonderful show while you can – tickets are selling fast as this is *Rock the Planet's* last month in the UK.

B Book to see *Rock the Planet* for an experience to remember. Check the website for great prices for student groups.

C You won't often see something as good as *Rock the Planet* – and with extra performers from America, the sound is even better than ever!

D After its success in several countries around the world, *Rock the Planet* has now opened in the UK!

Part 4

Questions 16–20

Five sentences have been removed from the text below.
For each question, choose the correct answer.
There are three extra sentences which you do not need to use.

A day in the life of an astronaut

Italian astronaut Samantha Cristoforetti talks about daily life on the International Space Station (ISS).

For the last few months, my home has been the International Space Station, orbiting 400 km above the surface of the earth, at 25,000 km per hour. We took off in a Russian Soyuz spaceship from Kazakhstan, and the flight to the Space Station took six hours. **16** ______ I felt incredibly excited.

There are two Americans, three Russians, and me. **17** ______ Fortunately, we all get on well. The day starts for everyone at 7 a.m. There's no gravity up here, so every morning I float through the cabin to attend our daily planning conference, or DPC. **18** ______ It usually lasts a few minutes. After it's finished, we speak to space centres around the world, including Houston (USA), Munich (Germany) and Tsukuba (Japan).

Then we have breakfast: oatmeal, eggs and coffee. In the past, astronauts had to suck food out of tubes. Nowadays, astronauts' food is served in special individual boxes with covers. **19** ______ Life has become much easier for astronauts over the years.

Our dinner is at around 7.30 p.m. My meals were prepared by an Italian chef on Earth before I left, and they're delicious. However, I do exchange a lot of food with my three colleagues from Russia.

20 ______ Their lentil and vegetable soup is also really good. Of course I miss fresh food, but a cargo spaceship comes once a month with fresh fruit. When I get back down to Earth, I know I'll miss this place.

A	I'm the only woman in this group.
B	That was a very long time to live in space.
C	People often ask what food tastes like in space.
D	This stops everything floating away while we eat!
E	On the other hand, the ISS is a perfect environment to do scientific experiments.
F	That's the meeting where we discuss what needs to be done during the day.
G	They like my desserts, and they have a dark bread that I love.
H	I'll never forget looking through the window and seeing it for the first time.

Part 5

Questions 21–26

For each question, choose the correct answer.

The world's largest school

City Montessori School in Lucknow, India, is the world's largest school. Nearly 50,000 pupils **(21)** .... classes there every day, and the school **(22)** .... nearly 4,000 staff, including teachers, cleaners, and electricians. The students learn traditional subjects such as geography and maths, and also discuss topics like world peace.

Dr Jagdish Gandhi set **(23)** .... the school in 1959. It was hard work, and at first, he had to **(24)** .... people to send their children to the school. But now, students come to him from all over the city.

At such a large school, pupils have to work hard to get **(25)** .... by the teachers. One pupil says: 'If you're chosen for a school team, you can certainly feel **(26)** .... of that.' Another pupil explains what he likes best: 'Being at the world's largest school means you can make lots of friends.'

21	**A** arrive	**B** attend	**C** go	**D** study
22	**A** employs	**B** receives	**C** gets	**D** owns
23	**A** in	**B** off	**C** out	**D** up
24	**A** explain	**B** hope	**C** persuade	**D** suggest
25	**A** thought	**B** looked	**C** noticed	**D** talked
26	**A** good	**B** proud	**C** positive	**D** happy

Part 6

Questions 27–32

For each question, write the correct answer.
Write **one** word for each gap.

A wildlife boat tour

When I was on holiday with my parents, we went on a wildlife tour. The trip involved sailing round some islands off the coast, not too far **(27)** .... our hotel. Some other guests had been on the tour, and recommended it to my parents, who immediately decided we should go.

In the morning our guide, Jake, picked us **(28)** .... in his boat and off we went. Jake knew lots about the wildlife on the islands and we saw everything we were hoping to, apart from one bird, called a harrier, which didn't appear. But that didn't matter **(29)** .... we saw many other amazing birds.

My parents especially liked the fact that **(30)** .... were very few people on the tour. Jake had time to answer all our questions, so we felt we learnt **(31)** .... than we'd expected. And we agreed this wildlife experience was **(32)** .... of the best we'd ever had.

WRITING (45 minutes)

Part 1

You **must** answer this question.
Write your answer in about **100 words** on the answer sheet.

Question 1

Read this email from your English teacher Mr Smith and the notes you have made.

EMAIL

From: Mr Smith
To: English class
Subject: End-of-term party

Dear English class,

Next month, we'll have our final English lesson of the term, so I'd like to organise a party for that day. What do you think of this idea?

Awesome!

We could either use the classroom or go to the park. Which place would be better for the party?

Explain which would be better

Can you suggest any fun activities for practising English during the party?

Suggest …

Also, it would be great if everyone could bring something to the party – please let me know what you can bring.

Offer …

Many thanks,

James Smith

Write your **email** to Mr Smith using **all the notes**.

Part 2

Choose **one** of these questions.
Write your answer in about **100 words** on the answer sheet.

Question 2

You see this announcement on an English-language website for young people.

> **Articles wanted!**
>
> Many people have friends who don't go to the same school as they do.
>
> What are the advantages of having friends who go to a different school?
>
> Is it difficult to keep in touch with friends if you don't see them at school?
>
> We'll publish the best articles answering these questions!

Write your **article**.

Question 3

Your English teacher has asked you to write a story.
Your story must begin with this sentence.

Ben and his father got off the plane and left the airport.

Write your **story**.

LISTENING (approximately 30 minutes)

Part 1

Questions 1–7

For each question, choose the correct answer.

---

1 Which book does the girl recommend to the boy?

A

B

C

2 How does the girl usually get to school?

A

B

C

3 Which is the girl's favourite photo?

A

B

C

4 Who will be on the TV programme today?

A

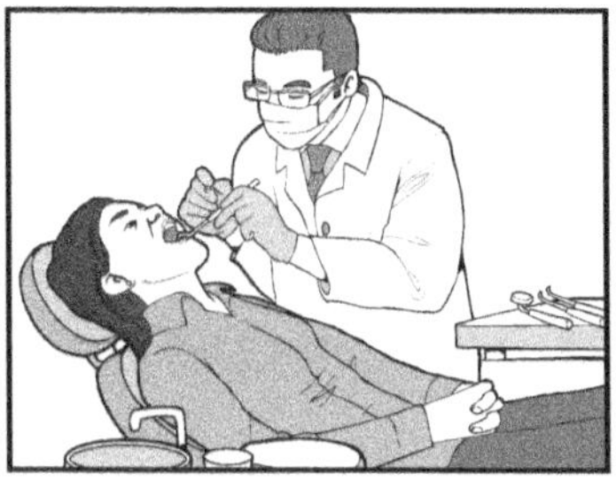

B

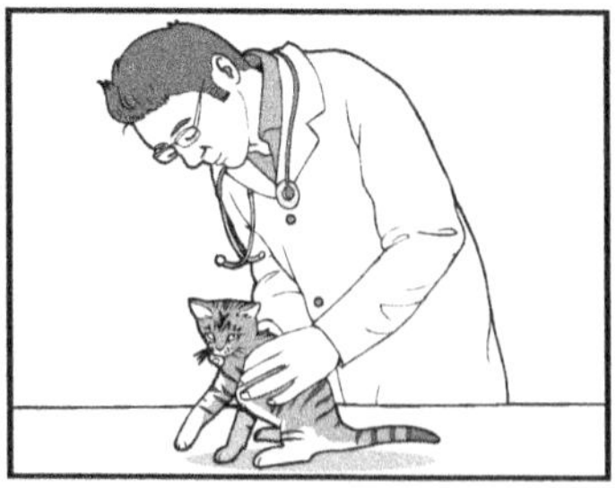

C

5 What are the brother and sister going to put in the room?

A

B

C

6 When will the school be able to use the pool?

A

B

C

7 What will the girl send to her aunt?

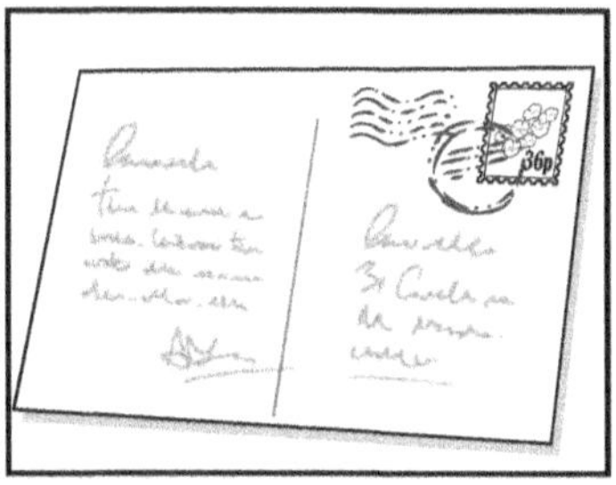

A

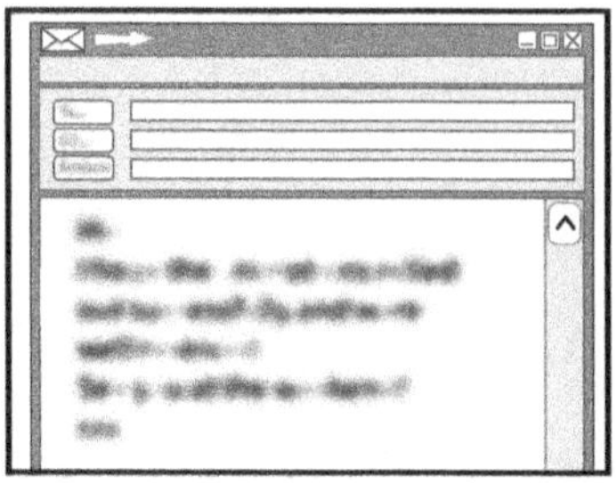

B

C

Part 2

Questions 8–13

For each question, choose the correct answer.

---

8 You will hear two friends talking in a shoe shop.
What does the boy like best about the trainers he wants to buy?

A They're reduced in price.

B They're a fashionable colour.

C They're comfortable to wear.

9 You will hear two friends talking about a sailing course they went on.
The girl thinks that

A one instructor was better than the others.

B they didn't make enough progress.

C the race on the last day was unfair.

10 You will hear two friends talking about a new computer game.
They agree that the best way of finding out about new games is through

A friends.

B the internet.

C special magazines.

11 You will hear a boy telling his friend about a football match.
Why is it postponed?

A Several members of the team aren't able to play.

B The weather today isn't suitable for playing football.

C The pitch isn't in good enough condition.

12 You will hear two friends talking about a new podcast.
What do they agree about it?

A It's good for finding out about fashion.

B It's presented in an unusual way.

C It's more interesting than most podcasts.

13 You will hear two friends talking about their holidays.
They agree that

A it's good to have time to relax on holiday.

B the best way to go on holiday is by plane.

C the coast is better than the mountains for holidays.

Part 3

Questions 14–19

For each question, write the correct answer in the gap. Write **one** or **two words** or a **number** or a **date** or a **time**.

You will hear a teacher telling her students about a trip to a museum.

City Museum trip

The first event will be a talk which lasts around **(14)** .... minutes.

The email address to send questions to is **(15)** .... @museum.org.

Groups of students will be able to hold some **(16)** .... which are on display.

In the Technology Centre, students will use **(17)** .... to learn more about ancient objects.

At the end of the visit, there will be a **(18)** ....

After the trip, students will create **(19)** .... for other students to look at.

Part 4

Questions 20–25

For each question, choose the correct answer.

You will hear an interview with a boy called Noah Kelly, who is talking about his love of horse riding.

20 Noah started horse riding because

A he was trying to be more active.

B he thought it seemed enjoyable.

C he wanted to lose his fear of animals.

21 What is unusual about the horse-riding club that Noah goes to?

A the people who ride there

B its opening hours

C its location

22 Noah says that his riding teacher

A knows what to expect from each horse.

B makes sure that riders help each other.

C finds ways to make each lesson fun.

23 How has Noah benefitted from horse riding?

A He's become a more organised person.

B He's become more patient.

C He's become fitter.

24 Noah says that horse-riding competitions are

A a lot of hard work.

B a good place to make friends.

C easier for people who have their own horse.

25 When he's older, Noah would like to

A enter races.

B work as a horse trainer.

C encourage more children to ride.

Test 3

READING (45 minutes)

Part 1

Questions 1–5

For each question, choose the correct answer.

1

This morning's chemistry lesson has moved because the Science laboratory is needed for staff training today. Wait in Room 197 until your teacher arrives and tells you where to go for your class.

A The chemistry teacher will wait for students in Room 197 today.

B Today's chemistry lesson will not be in the science laboratory.

C The chemistry lesson today will be watched by staff as part of their training.

2

Any books borrowed from the library must be returned by the last day of term. Library staff will then take your name off the list of students who still need to return books.

A Students who borrowed books must take them back by the end of term.

B There is a list of all students who have borrowed books this term.

C Students who want to keep books during the holidays must tell library staff.

3

08:21

Aidan
There are terrible traffic jams today, so I can't drive to school to pick you up as usual. Why don't you walk home rather than try to get a bus? It'll be quicker.
Mum

Aidan's mother is

A explaining why she will get to Aidan's school later than usual today.

B reminding Aidan that he was going to catch a bus home today.

C suggesting how Aidan should go home after school today.

4

Message

To...

Subject:

Please fill in the camping trip form, entering any food you need to avoid and ticking the activities you'd like to try. Remember it must be signed by your parents.

A Parents who are coming on the trip should sign the form.

B Students should choose what they want to do on the trip.

C Students should say what they'd prefer to eat during the trip.

5

Weekend babysitter needed!
Earn a little money looking after our two young children.
Must be over 15 – suitable for school student. Previous experiences unnecessary, but must be reliable and responsible.

People should only apply for this job if they

A are old enough.

B know a lot about babysitting.

C are still at school.

Part 2

Questions 6–10

For each question, choose the correct answer.

The people below all want to spend a day at a beach during their summer holidays.
On the opposite page there are descriptions of eight beaches.
Decide which beach would be the most suitable for the people below.

6  Joe's family want to go fishing in the morning. His parents would like to spend their afternoon learning about the history of the area while Joe takes part in a sports activity with other teenagers.

7  Tom and his father are very good surfers and are looking for a beach with challenging waves. They'd also like to do some other water sports and want to eat some fresh fish for dinner.

8  Zara and her family are interested in seeing ocean wildlife. The children would like to try surfing and they all want to keep their afternoon free for lying on the beach.

9  Jinnie's family need a beach with safe swimming areas for her younger sister, near a café offering good fish lunches. They want plenty of space so they can enjoy playing games together.

10  Matt and his family all want to go to a popular beach where they can watch an outdoor show or concert as well as do some fun activities.

Best beaches for a day out

A Tantsin Beach

Tantsin Beach is one of the biggest sandy beaches in the area – suitable for all ages. The beach resort overlooks the bay, which is full of colourful fish and is popular for kayaking. There is a small, calm section of the bay with lifeguards to watch the swimmers, and also several eating places serving local fish dishes all day long.

B Eastlee Beach

Walking on the sand, listening to the waves and passing the wonderful selection of coffee shops and fish restaurants, it is easy to see why Eastlee Beach is so popular. Visitors love taking boat trips around the bay to see the historic lighthouse. Afternoon surfing lessons are also on offer for teenagers.

C Hatton Beach

Lively and popular, with excellent restaurants serving locally-caught fish, Hatton Beach is a great place for surfing, though not suitable for beginners. The beach's sandy dunes lead down to several surfing, fishing, diving and water-skiing spots that are considered to be some of the finest in the area.

D Dunley Town Beach

On a trip to Dunley Town Beach, visitors will not only see the ocean and bay, but also a 14th-century castle on the hill. This fishing town has a quiet family beach, and classical concerts are held in the castle's Great Hall most evenings.

E North Beach

On this part of the coast, sunbathers, sand sculptors and in the summer months, whale watchers all enjoy the sand and sea. North Beach is a good place to have a surfing lesson in the morning, when the waves are smaller. In front of the beach clubhouse there are fun games and activities for children and teenagers to enjoy.

F Manou Beach

Manou Beach, with its seafront cafés and hotels, is popular with families. The sea is not suitable for swimming or water sports, but beach volleyball matches are organised for different age groups all through the day. Take a trip on a boat to try and catch salmon out at sea (we'll always be back before lunch time), take a dolphin-watching cruise, or visit the town museum.

G Maryland Beach

As the largest sandy beach along the coast, Maryland Beach is the West Coast's top vacation spot. The whole area is busy with summertime action: wonderful places for water sports, a water park, games for all ages, and even live entertainment on the beach.

H Kaloa Beach

Located on the East Coast, Kaloa has a magnificent beach. With its soft white sand, palm trees and clear, calm blue water, this beach is a natural choice for surf lovers, water sports enthusiasts and families in search of safe, sandy fun and games.

Part 3

Questions 11–15

For each question, choose the correct answer.

The teenage snowboarder

15-year-old Vanessa Hanson writes about her sport.

I was born in Denver, USA, and started snowboarding aged eight when my dad took me to a resort in the mountains, about two hours from Denver. The hill looked unbelievably steep and scary, so my dad had to do a lot of persuading to get me on a board. Because I was so young, I hadn't even thought of asking him if I could start snowboarding, but he was already into it and wanted me to love it too – he made it look so simple. And in the end, I managed just fine.

After this experience, it wasn't long before I'd developed a love of the sport and had improved my ability too. I started competing aged ten. Some people enter loads of competitions and end up getting bored of snowboarding, but my love of taking part, and winning too, if I'm honest, has got stronger as I've gotten older, which always helps me to push myself harder. I enjoy not having a fixed plan, and sometimes this goes well, like when I became the first female ever to get a perfect 100 at a local competition. I wasn't sure I'd even attempt the jumps that got me this score until I actually set off. That achievement increased my trust in my own abilities.

During the summer, I focus on training and my studies while there's no snow. Although I train daily, it's nice not having to stick to quite a strict diet like I do in the winter. I also get to spend lots of time with my friends then. It's the best way of dealing with not being able to do what I love so much and what I'm really good at.

I have to think carefully about my future. Snowboarding is such a huge part of my life now, but I also feel it's important to have something else I can do, just in case I don't succeed as a professional snowboarder or if I get injured. I'm wondering whether becoming a doctor is a possibility, if my active life allows time for doing a college degree. It's impossible to imagine myself growing tired of the sport, but I can't go on snowboarding my whole life.

11 Just before Vanessa snowboarded down a hill for the first time, she felt

A worried she was too young.

B nervous about doing it.

C keen to copy her father.

D pleased to be allowed to do it.

12 What does Vanessa say about taking part in competitions?

A She expects too much of herself.

B She sometimes loses interest.

C She always plans for them carefully.

D She enjoys them more and more.

13 In the summer, Vanessa enjoys

A the good weather where she lives.

B not having to train regularly.

C being able to eat whatever she likes.

D having plenty of time to do her schoolwork.

14 Vanessa says that in the future, snowboarding

A may not be her main career.

B will be a way for her to make a lot of money.

C might not always be interesting for her.

D will help her stay fit and healthy.

15 What would Vanessa say to one of her friends?

A I love snowboarding, but it's a shame I have so many accidents.

B I'm pleased that I'm more confident now. I hope this will help me, whatever I decide to do.

C I'm so happy to be a champion snowboarder like Dad – but I think he enjoys the sport more than I do.

D I'm sorry I've never been able to see you that much, even during the summer holidays.

Part 4

Questions 16–20

Five sentences have been removed from the text below.
For each question, choose the correct answer.
There are three extra sentences which you do not need to use.

Freezing food to keep it fresh

Inventor and businessman Clarence Birdseye was born in New York, on December 9, 1886. From a young age, he was interested in animals and plants and in 1909, Birdseye enrolled at university to study biology. **16** ______ Instead he took a job working for the US government as a naturalist in the frozen north of Canada.

When he was working in Labrador in 1912, Birdseye watched local people fishing through holes cut in an icy lake. **17** ______ He noticed that they could then be kept for long periods and, when the families wanted some to eat, they could defrost them without losing any of the freshness or flavour. Birdseye realised that cooling food very quickly was the key to success when freezing it. **18** ______ In warmer climates, people had experimented with freezing food by cooling it slowly. When food is frozen in this way, long sharp crystals of ice, shaped like knives, start to grow inside it. These cut into the food, causing it to break up when defrosted. **19** ______ Then he began to wonder how this freezing method might work with fresh vegetables and other foods as well as fish and meat.

When Birdseye returned to the US, he invented a machine which pressed food between two very cold metal plates. By 1930, it was ready to go into production. However, home freezers were very rare at this time. **20** ______ It was another 25 years before Birdseye's invention was widely used.

A	This was easy, of course, in very cold environments.
B	It took Birdseye eight years to work out how to cool food quickly enough to stop them forming.
C	He always came top of his university class.
D	As a result, few people wanted to buy frozen food.
E	They didn't catch many fish because they couldn't keep them fresh.
F	However, he was unable to afford the teaching fees, and had to leave.
G	For example, they were taken to nearby towns.
H	As they pulled out fish, these immediately froze in the extremely cold air.

Part 5

Questions 21–26

For each question, choose the correct answer.

The tallest trees in the world

The tallest trees in the world are called redwoods and they grow in California. These trees can **(21)** .... reach heights of around 91 metres. Among the enormous redwoods, one giant tree beats them all. This tree was discovered and measured in 2006. The National Park Service then **(22)** .... that at 115.7 metres, it was the tallest tree in the world. Now it is so famous that it even has a name, 'Hyperion'. In California there are other giant redwoods which are just a little shorter than Hyperion. The exact **(23)** .... of many of these enormous trees is kept secret to prevent them from being **(24)** ....

A **(25)** .... redwood tree lives for 500 to 700 years, although some have been found that are more than 2,000 years old. The National Park Service says that the redwoods' great height is **(26)** .... due to the climate in California; there is heavy rain every year and the temperatures are mild.

21	**A** clearly	**B** easily	**C** obviously	**D** luckily
22	**A** answered	**B** announced	**C** told	**D** spoke
23	**A** location	**B** route	**C** destination	**D** point
24	**A** wasted	**B** damaged	**C** worn	**D** injured
25	**A** familiar	**B** usual	**C** general	**D** typical
26	**A** mainly	**B** extremely	**C** properly	**D** finally

Part 6

Questions 27–32

For each question, write the correct answer.
Write **one** word for each gap.

School Jazz Band

Do you play a jazz instrument – maybe the trumpet, guitar or drums? Do you want to have some musical fun with other students in the school **(27)** .... have similar interests to yours? If you do, come and join us on Tuesdays after school in the music room. At the moment, there are eight of us playing quite a wide range of instruments. We're having such **(28)** .... great time and Mr Jones is an amazing jazz teacher, but we need more people, especially electric guitarists!

We're hoping **(29)** .... perform in the end-of-term show and Mr Jones said he'll deal **(30)** .... all the technical arrangements and the sound system, which is great!

Either come and ask me **(31)** .... more details during one of the lunch breaks, **(32)** .... just turn up on the day. But don't forget to bring your instrument! See you there!

Sam (from the School Jazz Band)

WRITING (45 minutes)

Part 1

You **must** answer this question.
Write your answer in about **100 words** on the answer sheet.

Question 1

Read this email from your English-speaking friend Alex and the notes you have made.

EMAIL

From: Alex

Subject: Next weekend's party

Hi

I'm so glad you can come to my party next weekend. I'm really excited about it!

Me too!

My parents are going to provide drinks for everybody, but I'm asking everyone to bring some food with them to the party. Can you bring a chocolate cake?

No, but ...

I think it would be fun if everyone could dress in special clothes for the party, like an animal or a famous person. What do you think?

Tell Alex

Also, I'll organise some games for us to play at the party. What's a good game that we can all play together?

Suggest ...

See you next weekend.

Alex

Write your **email** to Alex using **all the notes**.

Part 2

Choose **one** of these questions.
Write your answer in about **100 words** on the answer sheet.

Question 2

You see this announcement in an English-language magazine.

Articles wanted!

Tell us about a place that you really like in the area where you live.
Why do you like it? When do you go there? Is this place popular with other people too?

We'll publish the most interesting article answering these questions from each country!

Write your **article**.

Question 3

Your English teacher has asked you to write a story.
Your story must begin with this sentence.

Everybody clapped when I walked onto the stage.

Write your **story**.

LISTENING (approximately 30 minutes)

Part 1

Questions 1–7

For each question, choose the correct answer.

---

1 What has the boy lost?

A

B

C

2 Which painting won first prize in the competition?

A

B

C

3 Which activity is available at the sports centre next Saturday?

A

B

C

4 What does the girl need to buy?

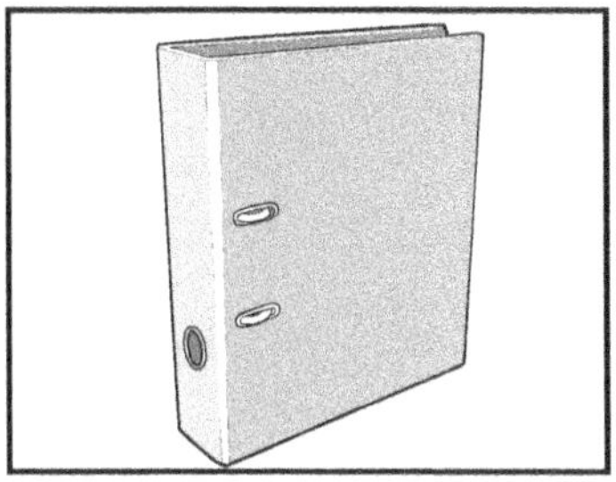

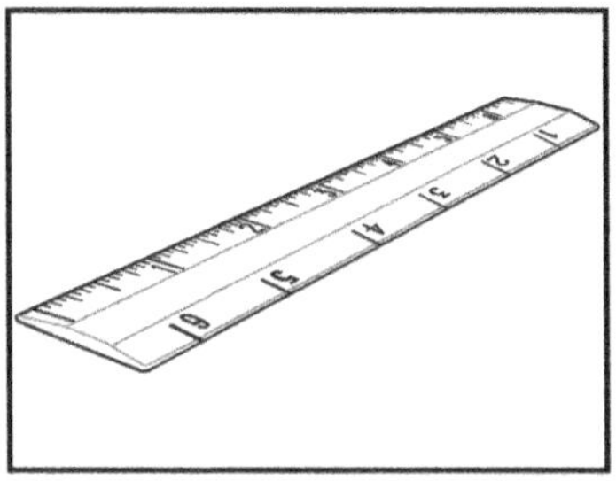

A **B** **C**

5 Where did the boy leave his sports bag?

A **B** **C**

6 Where are the boy and girl going on Saturday?

A **B** **C**

7 Which job is the new class project about?

A **B** **C**

Part 2

Questions 8–13

For each question, choose the correct answer.

---

8 You will hear a brother and sister talking about a school trip to a museum.
How does the boy feel about it?

A annoyed because he is unable to go

B excited about seeing all the new exhibitions

C confident that he will have a good time

9 You will hear a boy telling his friend about his new phone.
What does the boy like best about the phone?

A It has a nice appearance.

B It has a large amount of memory.

C It has a good camera.

10 You will hear two friends talking about a thunderstorm the day before.
What did the girl do?

A She found a way to avoid it.

B She went home quickly.

C She enjoyed watching it.

11 You will hear a boy telling a friend about his new bike.
What change is the boy most pleased about?

A He is spending less on transport.

B He feels more independent.

C He has got much fitter.

12 You will hear two friends talking about a film they have seen together.
They agree that

A the music was boring.

B the story was confusing.

C the interval was unnecessary.

13 You will hear two friends talking about a football club they play for.
They agree that

A their coach has a very serious attitude.

B their pitch needs some improvements.

C their team shirt should be a different colour.

Part 3

Questions 14–19

For each question, write the correct answer in the gap. Write **one** or **two words** or a **number** or a **date** or a **time**.

You will hear a boy giving a class presentation about a two-day trip he went on to a place called Sidelli.

Trip to Sidelli

Day One

Visit to: an ancient **(14)** .... by the sea

Guided tour: ruins of a **(15)** .... on a hill

Lunch: beside a **(16)** ....

Visit to: **(17)** .... Valley

Day Two

Most popular morning activity: **(18)** ....

Afternoon tour: a factory that makes: **(19)** ....

Part 4

Questions 20–25

For each question, choose the correct answer.

You will hear an interview with a girl called Jenna who went on a driving experience day for teenagers at a race track.

20 Why did Jenna go on the driving experience day?

- **A** A friend recommended it to her.
- **B** Someone gave her a ticket for her birthday.
- **C** Her brother said she could go instead of him.

21 How did Jenna feel when she arrived at the race track?

- **A** pleased to meet an instructor she'd heard of
- **B** surprised there were so few other drivers
- **C** disappointed by the car she was going to drive

22 While Jenna was watching the video before driving, she

- **A** suddenly felt nervous about what she was about to do.
- **B** almost changed her mind about going out in a car.
- **C** wished she had time to practise before going on the track.

23 When she was out on the race track, Jenna felt

- **A** excited to recognise the track from a computer game.
- **B** annoyed that she couldn't go faster.
- **C** confused by the car's controls.

24 Jenna says that she was unhappy about

- **A** how tired she felt after driving.
- **B** how long she was allowed to drive for.
- **C** how powerful the car was.

25 What would Jenna do differently if she drove again?

- **A** ask more questions about driving techniques
- **B** listen more carefully to all the instructions
- **C** try to remember each part of the race track

Test 4

READING (45 minutes)

Part 1

Questions 1–5

For each question, choose the correct answer.

1

Julia wants Kira to

A wait for her so they can go to lunch together.

B hurry up because she doesn't want to miss lunch.

C get to the canteen before it closes in 20 minutes.

2

Trainers must not be worn in classrooms. Please remove them and change back into normal shoes after sports lessons before you go back to your classroom.

A Do not bring your trainers to school.

B Take off your trainers when the sports class is over.

C Please change into the correct shoes in your classroom.

3

Student volunteers

Volunteers needed to work with other students for between one and four hours per week on coursework they're finding difficult. If you're willing to help, contact the school secretary.

Who should contact the school secretary?

A students who need help with their coursework

B students who want to help other students

C teachers who want to help students

4

Very reasonable second-hand mountain bike. One previous careful owner. Excellent condition.
For pictures, please contact me martin.999@nowmail.com

Why does Martin want people to contact him?

A in order to help him to buy a second-hand bike

B to share ideas about the best ways to look after a bike

C so that he can send them photos of the bike he wants to sell

5

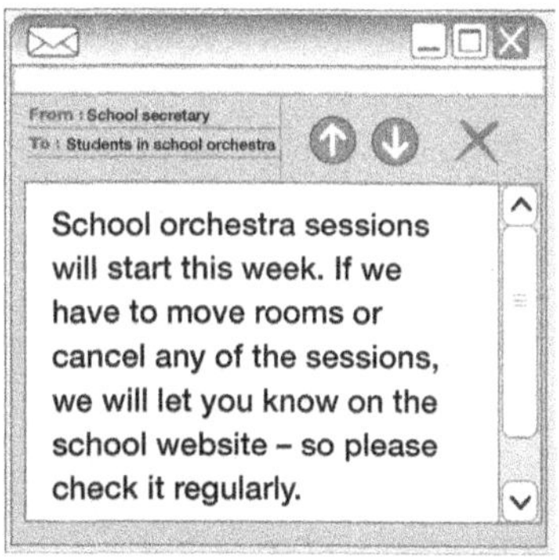

From : School secretary
To : Students in school orchestra

School orchestra sessions will start this week. If we have to move rooms or cancel any of the sessions, we will let you know on the school website – so please check it regularly.

A Students must not miss any of the orchestra sessions.

B The orchestra sessions will be in a different room each week.

C Students should look at the website in case there are any changes.

Part 2

Questions 6–10

For each question, choose the correct answer.

The people below all want to visit an ice cream factory with their families.
On the opposite page there are descriptions of eight ice cream factories.
Decide which factory would be the most suitable for the people below.

6 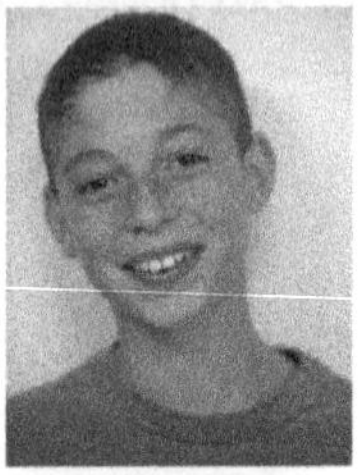

Sandro wants to visit a factory where they'll organise something special for his birthday, and where he'll see everything that's involved in producing ice cream. His parents want to spend some time outdoors during their visit.

7 

Jana's family would like to go to a factory that makes ice cream using traditional methods. Jana wants to try out different activities there, and make something that she can take home.

8 

Kem wants to see a factory that cares about its effects on the environment, and would like to find out how new flavours are invented. His dad enjoys visiting historically interesting buildings.

9 

Luisa would like to create her own ice cream using a variety of ingredients. Her mum wants to try other products the factory makes, and find something to entertain Luisa's small sister.

10 

Matty would like to visit a factory where they produce ice cream with unusual flavours, and buy a souvenir there. His mum wants to find out about the history of the company.

Ice cream factories

A **Frida's** farm isn't only famous for top-quality ice cream, but home-made cakes too – taste a range of them while you're here! Have a go at making ice cream yourself, adding whatever you fancy, from chocolate to vegetables! A perfect birthday activity – and there's an indoor playground for young children, too!

B **Henry's** has used the same methods for 50 years to produce first-class ice cream and celebration cakes! Based in an old country farmhouse, the building was the site of several interesting historical events. Visit the cows that produce our milk, and hear our plans for remaining environmentally friendly.

C **Denton's** has made ice cream since 1900, and is one of the country's favourites! The tour includes a talk about how Denton's was set up and how the business has developed over the years. The shop has great gifts and, in the café, try our strange but delicious ice cream varieties, including pea and blue cheese!

D At **Horley's**, we still make ice cream and cakes the same way it's been done for a hundred years. Help bake cakes in the visitors' kitchen, and record a Horley's ad on a DVD you can keep! Visit the beautiful 18th-century farmhouse, and meet the cows that produce our milk!

E At **Carswell's**, visitors will enjoy walking through the huge gardens and young children will love the animals at Pets' Corner. In the factory building, try our many flavours of ice cream, and get a souvenir from the fantastic shop – including some free ice cream!

F **Giulio's** factory is famous for its beautiful gardens and fantastic children's activities! Come and watch how ice cream is made, starting with collecting the milk. See machines turn it into ice cream, and finally, eat some! And if it's an important celebration, we'll make an ice-cream cake just for you!

G **Vascombe's** has made ice cream for 100 years – and it's always been delicious! See everything we do – from caring for our animals and the surrounding environment, to producing a variety of popular ice cream flavours! Try our delicious cakes and ice cream, and get a souvenir T-shirt to take home with you!

H **Jacobson's** is based in what was once the largest cotton factory in the area, designed by a well-known 19th-century architect. The factory now operates completely on wind power, and has won prizes for its recycling methods. Visit the lab where food scientists develop delicious and unusual flavours, and try making your own ice cream!

Part 3

Questions 11–15

For each question, choose the correct answer.

Challenge yourself!

15-year-old Kyle Washington writes about what he does in his free time.

I joined the National Youth Challenge (NYC) last year because I knew they went camping and sailing and taught skills like public speaking, and these were things I'd never done before. In the NYC you can do different activities to challenge yourself and you're always learning something. There are different levels, from beginner to advanced, run by adult volunteers called 'leaders'. When you complete each level you get a certificate.

When I first joined, my leader suggested that my first challenge should be helping to organise activities at a local children's club for two hours a week. I wasn't sure it was a good idea; I'd joined that same club when I was eight and I'd found it really difficult to make friends. I was quite shy then and all the other children already had their own friendship groups, so I'd stopped going after a couple of weeks. I decided to take up the challenge though, but only because I wanted my first NYC certificate.

Soon, however, I wanted to spend all my free time at the children's club. It meant a lot more to me than just getting the certificate. And when I finished the challenge, the NYC leader let me keep on volunteering at the club because I'd built up some great relationships with the children. Now I'm there for about four hours a week and I always really look forward to going.

Because of what I've learnt at the children's club, I've decided that when I finish school in three years' time I want to go to college to become a qualified youth worker – someone who works with children. It wasn't something I'd ever considered before starting at the club. In fact, I'd never thought about my future job, and the idea of youth work had never entered my mind. This has been my favourite part of the NYC so far and I've improved my own communication skills while at the same time helping others. I've got several other NYC certificates now and yes, one of them is for camping!

11 What was the main reason why Kyle joined the NYC?

A to improve some of his skills

B to reach the advanced level

C to become a volunteer leader

D to try new experiences

12 Why didn't Kyle want to start helping at the children's club?

A His memories of going there weren't very positive.

B He felt he was too shy to do a good job there.

C He didn't like the children there.

D None of his friends worked there.

13 Kyle still goes to the children's club because

A he needs to earn his next certificate.

B he enjoys spending time with the children.

C his leader asked him to carry on.

D his challenge is not yet finished.

14 Working at the children's club has helped Kyle to

A make a decision about his future career.

B go on his first camping expedition.

C get a place at college.

D achieve his dream of working with children.

15 What would Kyle's NYC leader say about him now?

A Kyle's learnt so much since he started with NYC. Now he just needs to learn to communicate better with young children.

B Even though Kyle's reduced the number of hours he works at the club, the work he does there is still extremely useful.

C Kyle's a good example of why people shouldn't be afraid of trying new things, and how this can bring unexpected benefits.

D Kyle's become a different person. He used to give up on his challenges but he doesn't do that any more.

Part 4

Questions 16–20

Five sentences have been removed from the text below.
For each question, choose the correct answer.
There are three extra sentences which you do not need to use.

Is too much messaging bad for us?

I've just read some interesting research in a magazine article about the amount of messaging that teenagers do. It seems that we send an average of 100 messages a day – that's 3,400 every month! The researchers say that this is very likely to have some big effects on parts of our lives. **16** ______ As we grow up, we start to rely less on them. But the research says that some teenagers message their parents up to 15 times a day. Some people might say that means that we depend on them too much. **17** ______

One thing did worry me a bit about the research though. It seems that for many of us, messaging doesn't end when the lights go out for the night. **18** ______ That's because if, like me, you keep the phone on after going to bed, the light shows when a new message comes in. This disturbs our sleep, and even though we're not completely awake, we'll often read the message and even reply. As a result, we might end up being rather bad-tempered in the morning. **19** ______

Of course, despite the fact that some of what I read in the article was rather negative, it's not all bad news. **20** ______ One advantage is that if you're feeling a bit shy, or just tired, and you don't want to communicate face-to-face, messaging is a great alternative. I think the main thing is that messaging can be a fantastic way to stay in touch as long as we don't do it too much. What do you think? Message me and let me know!!

A	That surely isn't the best way to start the day!
B	And, surprisingly, we often forget that it didn't!
C	Despite this difficulty, messaging can be much quicker than a conversation.
D	However, I think it's just nice to stay in touch.
E	Another reason is that often we just can't wait to see our friends.
F	There are plenty of good things about messaging too.
G	One of these, they say, is our connection with our parents.
H	Many of us message while we're doing other things, like homework.

Part 5

Questions 21–26

For each question, choose the correct answer.

The Titan Arum

We usually expect flowers to have an attractive smell. However, this isn't true of all of them. The flowering plant called the Titan Arum only produces flowers every ten years or so – but when it does, the smell is so **(21)** .... that most people say they can't stand being near the flower, unless they hold their noses. They say that it's the worst smell they have ever **(22)** ....

The plant, which can grow to over 100 cm tall, is able to produce heat. As this happens, the bad smell is created. But the smell does have a purpose. It's intended to encourage all kinds of insects to travel **(23)** .... distances to visit the flowers.

The flowers always **(24)** .... a lot of interest because they are produced so **(25)** .... Scientists wanting to study the plant need to **(26)** .... out their research before the flowers disappear again for another ten years.

21	**A** messy	**B** disgusting	**C** frightening	**D** painful
22	**A** experienced	**B** met	**C** realised	**D** felt
23	**A** far	**B** broad	**C** wide	**D** long
24	**A** aim	**B** offer	**C** demand	**D** attract
25	**A** rarely	**B** slightly	**C** hardly	**D** lately
26	**A** take	**B** find	**C** carry	**D** start

Part 6

Questions 27–32

For each question, write the correct answer.
Write **one** word for each gap.

A trip to the theatre

We had a class day out today. We went on a theatre trip **(27)** .... see Shakespeare's play Hamlet. A friend of mine, **(28)** .... has always been really into Shakespeare, had already told me the story. Basically, Hamlet discovers a terrible secret about his family, but he can't decide **(29)** .... to do about it. I won't say any more about the story, in case you decide to go and see it as well. I'd hate to spoil it for you! The only thing I didn't like about the play was **(30)** .... fact that it lasted four hours. For me, that was far **(31)** .... long, and the seats were quite uncomfortable. Afterwards, my mum asked me **(32)** .... I'd go and see another Shakespeare play. I said yes, I probably would, but I'd take a cushion next time!

WRITING (45 minutes)

Part 1

You **must** answer this question.
Write your answer in about **100 words** on the answer sheet.

Question 1

Read this email from your English-speaking friend Jo and the notes you have made.

EMAIL

From: Jo

Subject: Geography presentation

Hi

I'm glad we're going to do our school geography presentation together, because I know you're really good at geography! — *Thanks!*

The teacher said we can choose to tell the class about rivers or deserts for our presentation. Which do you think would be better? — *Explain*

What do you think we could do to make the presentation more interesting? — *Tell Jo*

We need to start planning the presentation soon! Can you come to my house on Tuesday evening after school? — *No, but …*

See you soon.

Jo

Write your **email** to Jo using **all the notes**.

Part 2

Choose **one** of these questions.
Write your answer in about **100 words** on the answer sheet.

Question 2

You see this announcement in an English-language magazine.

Articles wanted!

Free-time activities

Tell us about a free-time activity which is popular with young people in your country.
Why do people enjoy it so much?

Write an article answering these questions and we'll publish the most interesting ones on our website.

Write your **article**.

Question 3

Your English teacher has asked you to write a story.
Your story must begin with this sentence.

It was Jack's birthday and he was feeling very happy.

Write your **story**.

LISTENING (approximately 30 minutes)

Part 1

Questions 1–7

For each question, choose the correct answer.

---

1 Which instrument is the girl going to learn to play?

A

B

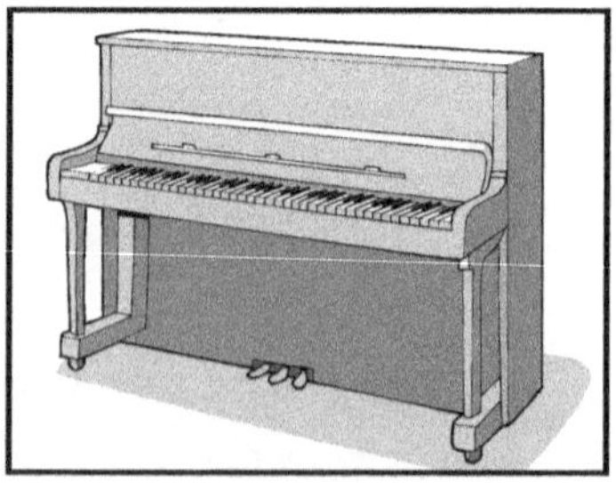

C

2 Which programme are they going to watch?

A

B

C

3 Which picture shows the girl's cousin?

A

B

C

4 Which part of the boy's leg is painful?

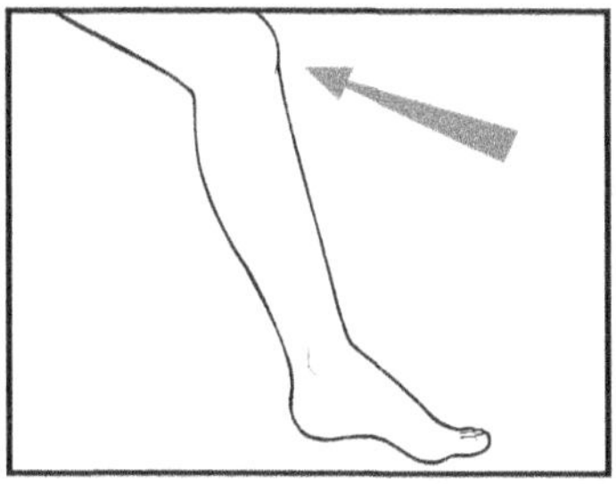

A

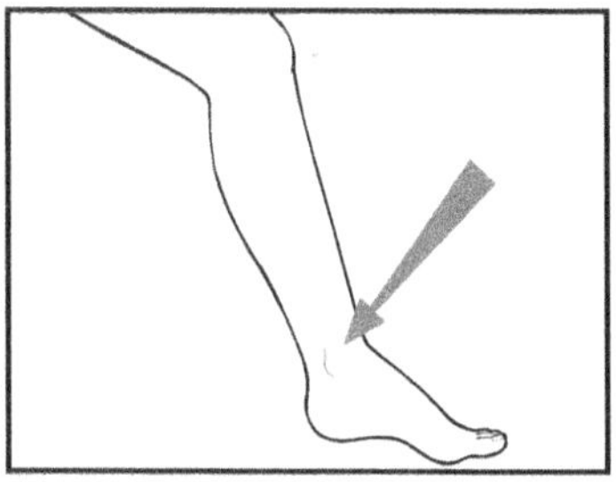

B

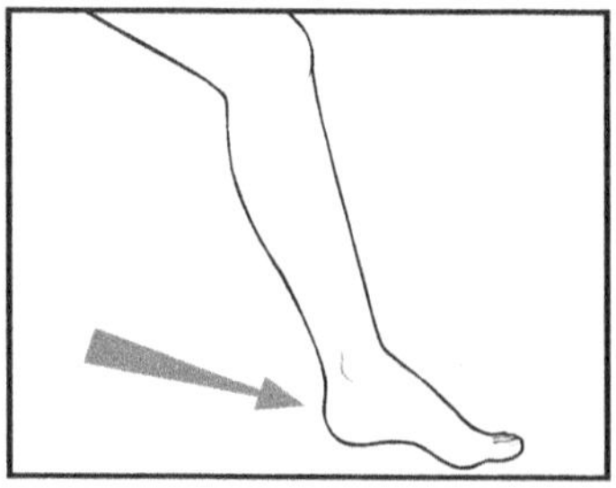

C

5 How much money should students take on the trip?

£8	£12	£24
A	**B**	**C**

6 Which picture is the teacher talking about?

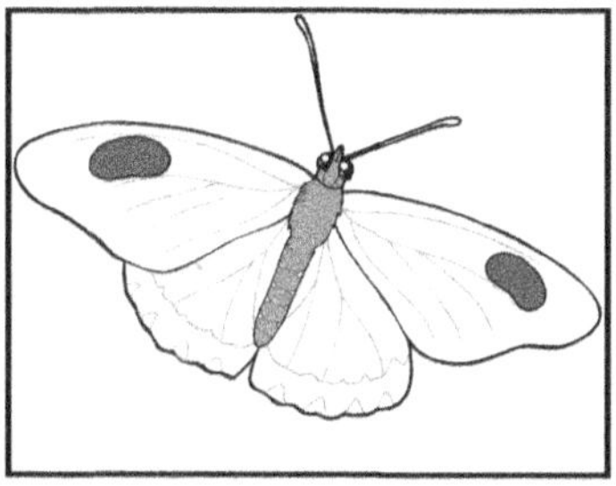

A

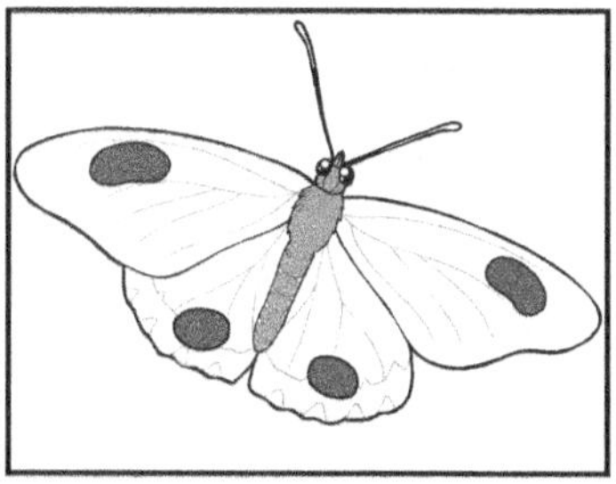

B

C

7 What has the girl learned how to make?

A

B

C

Part 2

Questions 8–13

For each question, choose the correct answer.

---

8 You will hear two friends talking about their school project.
Why is the girl interested in space travel?

A She wants to be an astronaut.

B She likes science fiction films.

C She enjoys studying physics.

9 You will hear two friends talking during a game of chess.
What do they agree about it?

A It isn't very exciting to play.

B It isn't easy to learn how to play.

C It isn't as much fun as playing computer games.

10 You will hear two friends talking in a fast food restaurant.
What does the woman say about her burger?

A It's smaller than she expected.

B It's more expensive than she expected.

C It's less tasty than she expected.

11 You will hear two friends talking about their history homework.
What does the girl think about it?

A There's a lot to do.

B It looks difficult.

C She needs some help.

12 You will hear a girl talking to a friend about becoming a member of a swimming team.
The girl feels

A worried about the effect of training on her studies.

B surprised that she was chosen for the team.

C confused by the arrangements for competitions.

13 You will hear two friends talking about a school trip to a river.
The boy thinks

A the trip costs too much.

B the river is too far away.

C the coach leaves too early.

Part 3

Questions 14–19

For each question, write the correct answer in the gap. Write **one** or **two words** or a **number** or a **date** or a **time**.

You will hear a student giving a talk about a trip to see some seabirds called puffins.

Trip to see puffins

Puffins are known as **(14)** .... by people in the local area.

Puffins can be funny to watch when they are moving on **(15)** ....

The puffins leave the islands during **(16)** ....

The islands' puffins build their nests in a similar way to **(17)** ....

Almost **(18)** .... puffins came to the islands last year.

Volunteers are necessary to **(19)** .... the puffins.

Part 4

Questions 20–25

For each question, choose the correct answer.

You will hear an interview with a girl called Jennifer Marsden, who is a comedian, someone who tells jokes in front of an audience.

20 Jennifer first realised she was good at telling jokes when she

A performed in a school show.

B met a well-known comedian.

C was trying to make her family laugh.

21 Jennifer says that she writes her funniest jokes by

A watching news stories on TV.

B getting ideas from other people.

C using her personal experiences.

22 How do Jennifer's classmates feel about her being a comedian?

A keen to learn similar skills

B proud of her success

C surprised by her ability

23 What is the most difficult situation Jennifer has faced on stage?

A forgetting what to say

B people shouting things

C nobody laughing at her jokes

24 Who does Jennifer say has helped her improve as a comedian most?

A her teachers

B other comedians

C audiences

25 Jennifer says that in the future, she will

A carry on performing.

B work in medicine.

C be a full-time comedian.

Draft

OFFICE USE ONLY - DO NOT WRITE OR MAKE ANY MARK ABOVE THIS LINE — Page 1 of 2

Cambridge Assessment English

Candidate Name		Candidate Number	
Centre Name		Centre Number	
Examination Title		Examination Details	
Candidate Signature		Assessment Date	

Supervisor: If the candidate is ABSENT or has WITHDRAWN shade here O

Preliminary for Schools Reading Candidate Answer Sheet

Instructions

Use a PENCIL (B or HB)

Rub out any answer you want to change with an eraser.

For Parts 1, 2, 3, 4 and 5:

Mark ONE letter for each answer.

For example: If you think A is the right answer to the question, mark your answer sheet like this:

0	A	B	C

Part 1

1	A	B	C
2	A	B	C
3	A	B	C
4	A	B	C
5	A	B	C

Part 2

6	A	B	C	D	E	F	G	H
7	A	B	C	D	E	F	G	H
8	A	B	C	D	E	F	G	H
9	A	B	C	D	E	F	G	H
10	A	B	C	D	E	F	G	H

Part 3

11	A	B	C	D
12	A	B	C	D
13	A	B	C	D
14	A	B	C	D
15	A	B	C	D

Part 4

16	A	B	C	D	E	F	G	H
17	A	B	C	D	E	F	G	H
18	A	B	C	D	E	F	G	H
19	A	B	C	D	E	F	G	H
20	A	B	C	D	E	F	G	H

Part 5

21	A	B	C	D
22	A	B	C	D
23	A	B	C	D
24	A	B	C	D
25	A	B	C	D
26	A	B	C	D

Continues over ➡

OFFICE USE ONLY - DO NOT WRITE OR MAKE ANY MARK BELOW THIS LINE — Page 1 of 2

Draft

Draft

OFFICE USE ONLY - DO NOT WRITE OR MAKE ANY MARK ABOVE THIS LINE

For Part 6:
Write your answers clearly in the spaces next to the numbers (27 to 32) like this:

0 ENGLISH

Write your answers in CAPITAL LETTERS.

Part 6		Do not write below here
27		27 1 0
28		28 1 0
29		29 1 0
30		30 1 0
31		31 1 0
32		32 1 0

OFFICE USE ONLY - DO NOT WRITE OR MAKE ANY MARK BELOW THIS LINE

Draft

You must write within the grey lines.

Write your answer for Part 1 below. Do not write on the barcodes.

Question 1

This section for use by Examiner only:

C	CA	O	L

* 0010446611102 *

You must write within the grey lines.

Answer only one of the two questions for Part 2.
Tick the box to show which question you have answered.
Write your answer below. Do not write on the barcodes.

Part 2	Question 2 ☐	Question 3 ☐

This section for use by Examiner only:

C	CA	O	L

* 0010446611103 *

Draft

OFFICE USE ONLY - DO NOT WRITE OR MAKE ANY MARK ABOVE THIS LINE — Page 1 of 1

Cambridge Assessment English

Candidate Name		Candidate Number	
Centre Name		Centre Number	
Examination Title		Examination Details	
Candidate Signature		Assessment Date	

Supervisor: If the candidate is ABSENT or has WITHDRAWN shade here O

Preliminary for Schools Listening Candidate Answer Sheet

Instructions

Use a PENCIL (B or HB). Rub out any answer you want to change with an eraser.

For Parts 1, 2 and 4:

Mark one letter for each answer. For example: If you think **A** is the right answer to the question, mark your answer sheet like this:

0 A B C

For Part 3:

Write your answers clearly in the spaces next to the numbers (14 to 19) like this:

0 ENGLISH

Write your answers in CAPITAL LETTERS.

Part 1	A	B	C
1	O	O	O
2	O	O	O
3	O	O	O
4	O	O	O
5	O	O	O
6	O	O	O
7	O	O	O

Part 2	A	B	C
8	O	O	O
9	O	O	O
10	O	O	O
11	O	O	O
12	O	O	O
13	O	O	O

Part 3		Do not write below here
14		14 1 O 0 O
15		15 1 O 0 O
16		16 1 O 0 O
17		17 1 O 0 O
18		18 1 O 0 O
19		19 1 O 0 O

Part 4	A	B	C
20	O	O	O
21	O	O	O
22	O	O	O
23	O	O	O
24	O	O	O
25	O	O	O

OFFICE USE ONLY - DO NOT WRITE OR MAKE ANY MARK BELOW THIS LINE — Page 1 of 1

Draft

Acknowledgements

The authors and publishers acknowledge the following sources of copyright material and are grateful for the permissions granted. While every effort has been made, it has not always been possible to identify the sources of all the material used, or to trace all copyright holders. If any omissions are brought to our notice, we will be happy to include the appropriate acknowledgements on reprinting and in the next update to the digital edition, as applicable.

Photographs

Key: T = Test, R = Reading, S = Speaking.

All the photographs are sourced from Getty Images.

T1 R P2: Yuripere's photo/Moment Open; Echo/Juice Images; Blue_Cutler/iStock/Getty Images Plus; J-Elgaard/iStock/Getty Images Plus; Callietat/iStock/Getty Images Plus; **T2 R P2:** PeopleImages/iStock/Getty Images Plus; Hero Images; Anna_Om/iStock/Getty Images Plus; blackwaterimages/E+; kali9/E+; **T3 R P2:** Juanmonino/E+; Maica/iStock/Getty Images Plus; Juanmonino/iStock/Getty Images Plus; Jbryson/iStock/Getty Images Plus; Jose Luis Pelaez Inc/Blend Images; **T4 R P2:** Yellow Dog Productions/Photographer's Choice; Westend61; Jose Luis Pelaez/Photodisc; Gary John Norman/Cultura/Getty Images Plus; nilimage/iStock/Getty Images Plus; **T1 S P2:** Robert Daly/Caiaimage; Moretti/Viant/Caiaimage; **T2 S P2:** Lumi Images/Robert Niedring; Peter Muller/Cultura; **T3 S P2:** Johner Images; Hero Images; **T4 S P2:** Caiaimage/Sam Edwards/OJO+; Judith Haeusler/Cultura.

Typeset by QBS Learning.

Audio production by Real Deal Productions and dsound recording Ltd.

Visual materials for the Speaking test

Test 1

Part 2

Task 1A

Task 1B

Test 1

Part 3

Task 1C

Things to take for a walk in the mountains

Test 2

Task 2A

Task 2B

Test 2

Part 3

Task 2C

Ways to find out about the history of the local area

Test 3

Task 3A

Task 3B

Test 3

Part 3

Task 3C

School project about fashion

Test 4

Task 4A

Task 4B

Test 4

Part 3

Task 4C

Activities to do on a long train journey

Caiaimage/Sam Edwards/Getty Imag